Jeff,

We are so happy for you and Laura!
You will be such wonderful parents.
Luke is so lucky to have you for a
father; you'll make such a great mentor,
coach and friend to the little guy.

Love,

Brian & Hannah

It's a Dad Thing

It's a Dad Thing

Fathoming the Phenomenon of Fatherhood

WILLOW CREEK PRESS

Published by Willow Creek Press, Inc.
P.O. Box 147, Minocqua, Wisconsin 54548

Photo Credits:
© ClassicStock/Masterfile; p2, p5, p7, p8, p11, p15, p19, p23, p24, p28, p31, p32, p35, p36, p39, p43, p44, p47, p48, p51, p52, p55, p56, p59, p63, p64, p67, p68, p72, p75, p76, p79, p80, p83, p84, p87, p91, p92, p95

Design: Donnie Rubo
Printed in Canada

Advice

My dad always used to tell me that if they challenge
you to an after~school fight. tell them you
won't wait—you can kick their ass right now.

~Cameron Diaz

Approval

Your folks are like God because you want to know
they're out there and you want them to approve
of your life, still you only call them when
you're in a crisis and need something.

~Chuck Palahniuk

Authority

All fathers are invisible in daytime; daytime is ruled by mothers and fathers come out at night. Darkness brings home fathers, with their real, unspeakable power. There is more to fathers than meets the eye.

~Margaret Atwood

Blame

Parenthood is the passing of a baton, followed by
a lifelong disagreement as to who dropped it.

~Robert Brault

Caprice

Parenthood is a lot easier to get into than out of.

~Bruce Lansky

Clarity

Sherman made the terrible discovery that men make about
their father sooner or later... that the man before him was not
an aging father but a boy, a boy much like himself, a boy who
grew up and had a child of his own and, as best he could, out of
a sense of duty and, perhaps love, adopted a role called Being
a Father so that his child would have something mythical and
infinitely important; a Protector, who would keep a lid on all
the chaotic and catastrophic possibilities of life.

~Tom Wolfe

Curmudgeon

My father hated radio, he could not wait for television
to be invented so he could hate that too.

~Peter De Vries

Daughters

The father of a daughter is nothing but a high~class
hostage. A father turns a stony face to his sons,
berates them, shakes his antlers, paws the ground,
snorts, runs them off into the underbrush, but when
his daughter puts her arm over his shoulder and says,
"Daddy, I need to ask you something," he is a
pat of butter in a hot frying pan.

~Garrison Keillor

Dilemma

A king, realizing his incompetence, can either
delegate or abdicate his duties. A father can
do neither. If only sons could see the paradox,
they would understand the dilemma.

~Marlene Dietrich

Discipline

A man's children and his garden both reflect the
amount of weeding done during the growing season.

~Unknown

Disdain

·••◄●►••·

If you have never been hated by your
child, you have never been a parent.

~Bette Davis

Division

···◄ ●►···

For thousands of years, father and son have stretched
wistful hands across the canyon of time, each eager to
help the other to his side, but neither quite able to desert
the loyalties of his contemporaries. The relationship is
always changing and hence always fragile; nothing
endures except the sense of difference.

~Alan Valentine

Dread

One night a father overheard his son pray: Dear
God, make me the kind of man my Daddy is. Later
that night, the father prayed, Dear God, make me
the kind of man my son wants me to be.

~Unknown

Education

Dad taught me everything I know. Unfortunately,
he didn't teach me everything he knows.

~Al Unser. Sr.

Evolution

There are three stages of a man's life: he believes
in Santa Claus, he doesn't believe in
Santa Claus, he is Santa Claus.

~Unknown

Examples

He didn't tell me how to live; he lived,
and let me watch him do it.

~Clarence Budington Kelland

Expectations

If you must hold yourself up to your children
as an object lesson, hold yourself up as
a warning and not as an example.

~George Bernard Shaw

Fear

The joys of parents are secret, and
so are their griefs and fears.

~Francis Bacon, Sr.

Heartbreak

Until you have a son of your own... you will never know the
joy, the love beyond feeling that resonates in the heart of
a father as he looks upon his son. You will never know the
sense of honor that makes a man want to be more than he is
and to pass something good and hopeful into the hands of his
son. And you will never know the heartbreak of the fathers
who are haunted by the personal demons that keep them
from being the men they want their sons to be.

~Kent Nerburn

Legacy

His heritage to his children wasn't words or posses[sions]
but an unspoken treasure—the treasure of his
example as a man and a father.

~Will Rodgers

ions,

...ild y...

...ll do the most to m...

~Mignon McLaughlin

Influence

Don't worry that children never listen to you;
worry that they are always watching you.

~Robert Fulghum

Heredity

If I chance to talk a little wild, forgive
me; I had it from my father.

~William Shakespeare

Love

The most important thing a father can do
for his children is to love their mother.

~Unknown

Memories

···◄●►···

When you have brought up kids, there are memories
you store directly in your tear ducts.

~Robert Brault

Nurturing

A man never stands as tall as
when he kneels to help a child.

~Knights of Pythagoras

Obedience

Children aren't happy with nothing to ignore.
And that's what parents were created for.

~Ogden Nash

Perspective

They didn't believe their father had ever been young;
surely even in the cradle he had been a very, very
small man in a gray suit, with a little dark
mustache and flat, incurious eyes.

~Richard Shattuck

Praise

When I was a kid, my father told me every day,
"You're the most wonderful boy in the world,
and you can do anything you want to."

~Jan Hutchins

Pride

It's only when you grow up and step back from him, or
leave him for your own career and your own home—
it's only then that you can measure his greatness
and fully appreciate it. Pride reinforces love.

~Margaret Truman

Priorities

My father used to play with my brother and me in
the yard. Mother would come out and say, "You're
tearing up the grass." "We're not raising grass," Dad
would reply. "We're raising boys."

~Harmon Killebrew

Protection

I cannot think of any need in childhood as
strong as the need for a father's protection.

~Sigmund Freud

Rebellion

A dramatic thing, the first time
you stand up to your dad.

~Lenny Kravitz

Responsibility

Some parents really bring their children up;
others let them down.

~Unknown

Revery

—•◀▶•—

My dad was the town drunk. Most of the time that's
not so bad; but New York City?

~Henny Youngman

Shock

When a child is born, a father is born. A mother is
born, too of course, but at least for her it's a gradual
process. Body and soul, she has nine months to get used
to what's happening. She becomes what's happening.
But for even the best~prepared father, it happens all
at once. On the other side of a plate~glass window, a
nurse is holding up something roughly the size of a
loaf of bread for him to see for the first time.

~Frederick Buechner

Sons

Don't wait to make your son a great man—
make him a great boy.

~Unknown

Stress

Children are a great comfort in your old age—
and they help you reach it faster, too.

~Lionel Kauffman

Struggle

The trouble with having a stubbornness contest with
your kids is that they have your stubbornness gene.

~Robert Brault

Technique

Spread the diaper in the position of the diamond with
you at bat. Then fold second base down to home and
set the baby on the pitcher's mound. Put first base
and third together, bring up home plate and pin the
three together. Of course, in case of rain, you gotta
call the game and start all over again.

~Jimmy Piersal

Vanity

A man's desire for a son is usually nothing but the wish
to duplicate himself in order that such a remarkable
pattern may not be lost to the world.

~Helen Rowland

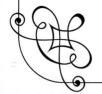

Violence

Never raise your hand to your kids.
It leaves your groin unprotected.

~Red Buttons

Wealth

Sometimes the poorest man leaves
his children the richest inheritance.

~Ruth E. Renkel

Wisdom

•••◀ ● ▶•••

It is a wise father that knows his own child.

~William Shakespeare

Youth

Why are men reluctant to become fathers?
They aren't through being children.

~Cindy Garner

The End